the brightened mind

the brightened mind

a simple guide to Buddhist meditation

AJAHN SUMANO BHIKKHU

QUEST

BOOKS

Theosophical Publishing House

Wheaton, Illinois • Chennai, India

Quest Books
Theosophical Publishing House
P. O. Box 270
Wheaton, IL 60187-0270

www.questbooks.net

Cover design by Drew Stevens

Library of Congress Cataloging-in-Publication Data

Sumano, Ajahn, Bhikkhu.
The Brightened Mind: A Simple Guide to Buddhist Meditation / Ajahn Sumano Bhikkhu.—First Quest Edition.
        pages   cm
ISBN 978-0-8356-0899-2
1. Meditation—Buddhism.   I. Title.

BQ5612.S915 2011
294.3'4435—dc22   2010046969

        5   4   3   2   1   *   11   12   13   14   15

Printed in the United States of America

JUN 2 1 2011

CONTENTS

Introduction   1

The Two Levels of Consciousness   11

The Universal Mind   25

The Need for Spiritual Education   35

Mind-Training Exercises   45
   Focus on Breathing   49
   Preparing the Body and the Mind   52
   The Mind-Fitness Technique   58

Summary   71

The Ultimate Goal   79

Contemplations for the Reader   87
   A Meditation on Loving-Kindness   89
   Reflections on Being   93
   Affirmation of Spiritual Friendship   103

About the Author   105

Introduction

Unless you have spent your life in some remote part of the world, like millions of other people you are very much aware of and becoming more concerned about the increasing danger of living in a modern society such as ours. You will have noticed feeling a bit more stressed when going about your daily activities, such as commuting to and from your home. Most likely, you have seen evidence of this danger in multicar collisions, motorcycle crashes, road-rage fights, police-car chases, vandalizing of private property, construction accidents, and a host of other troubles. Sad to say, such events are just a routine part of a typical day in almost any city. Most of the time, though, we can reduce our own risk simply by being prudent and more vigilant.

But there is a greater, far more menacing threat than what we encounter in our physical surroundings. It is destructive in ways that we can hardly imagine, because we cannot see its potential for causing us serious harm. In a manner of speaking, the world we inhabit (our neighborhoods, workplaces, local establishments, classrooms, and so on) has become a battleground for controlling our minds.

If we do not know how to protect ourselves with wise discernment, we are easy prey to mental and psychological assaults from the external influences of our neighbors, bosses, teachers, and the media, as well as the internal pressures of the ego, which will, in time, weaken our resistance. And, before we know it, with very little struggle, we will have unsuspectingly surrendered control of our mind—the most precious thing we have.

But we can take heart in the truths that life is an ongoing process of change and that each moment can be a potential turning point for us. Like this very moment, right now. If you, for example, are reading this book, know that it is your "boon" that led you to do so. That truth, on its own, is a huge advantage and a powerful ally that can further guide you to important knowledge crucial to your psychological and spiritual survival.

You will learn here all the information you will ever need to make your mind alert, vibrant, agile, powerful, and, most of all, vigilant against mental and psychological pressures vying for your attention. The ideas offered in these pages are simple and practical, although not necessarily easy to put into practice. Yet when applied with steadfast diligence they are certain to give you profound results. As with all things worthwhile, sincere and determined effort is the driving force that will activate the abundant benefits of a brightened mind.

The technique this book explains for establishing attention and alertness is one from which people of all ages and all lifestyles can benefit. It will prove to be extraordinarily useful for office employees, information-technology professionals, taxi drivers, teachers, students, street vendors, car washers, airline staff, or even someone who just sells popcorn at the movies. Whether you are in a business meeting, attending a high school class or college seminar, cooking dinner, or participating in a yoga lesson, the same fundamentals will come into play. The mind changes, but the nature of the mind remains the same.

The brightened mind is a mind that is able to make better choices. As we know from experience, our choices deeply impact our lives. They determine what we do, where we work, with whom we live, and the like. We should make decisions that are in harmony with our karma, personality, and life circumstances. And we should not allow our sensitivity and intelligence to be swayed by our impulsive and ill-considered hopes and dreams. Our lives can be grounded in reality, not by a script from a movie or some offhanded advice we ran across in a magazine.

Actually, the skills learned here will initiate in you an interest for understanding the mind (i.e., who you are). As your understanding increases, the spiritual aspect of your life will organically evolve. With this technique as a basis, you will be primed to develop the wisdom that will lead you to make several important distinctions:

- You will understand the difference between memorizing data and the manifestation of wisdom.

- You will understand the difference between the "good" and the "appropriate." *Good* as I mean it encompasses the prohibitions and precepts taught by all religions (such as not to kill, steal, or indulge in illicit sexual relationships), as well as the values and taboos of a particular culture. It also encompasses the life experiences—positive and negative—of a person. Our concept of the *good* is thus informed by the past, whereas the concept of *appropriate* applies only to the moment. What is appropriate is what needs to be done *now*! The action arises from pure, present-moment awareness, and that awareness is a world apart from memory and from our inclination to seek happiness and to avoid suffering. When, for instance, a mother lifts up a car by herself to pull her child out from under the wheels, she is functioning purely out of what is appropriate in the moment, without the imposition of memory, hesitation, or fear.

- You will become able to differentiate between feeling and thinking . . . and you will become able to understand from where each originates.

- You will be able to extract different aspects of the mind that include awareness and the object of awareness, positive mental states and negative ones.

- You will be able to recognize concentration (*samadhi*) from insight (*vipassana*) and the difference between shallow (mundane) happiness and unfettered (profound) happiness.

Opening and strengthening our minds is critical to how well we live our lives. With the skills you learn from meditation, you will see with time the changing conditions we face daily, but with a poised, cool, and compassionate heart.

The Two Levels
of Consciousness

Most of us assume the existence of just one level of consciousness, based on the only level we know and operate from. But the truth is that consciousness has two distinct modes: the ordinary and the extraordinary. The first mode is the mundane and superficial way we see and act in the world most of the time. The second mode is a concept beyond the realm of our ordinary comprehension that cannot be adequately described. Rather, we can know it for ourselves simply through direct experience. We might say that this second state is "that which is."

We will look into both these modes of consciousness so that we may become proficient in how they operate and, ultimately, learn how to use this knowledge to enhance the quality of our life.

First, we should understand that the mundane mind, under the authority of the "I-ego," is driven mainly by its desire for survival and comfort. It is, therefore, constantly mounted by fear—the fear of losing its dominant influence over our thinking process. In order to preserve and secure its position more firmly, it invents self-serving scenarios designed to entice our senses into buying its agenda. This ordinary mind cleverly uses materials drawn mainly from attractive memories of the past. It conjures up a fantasy future built out of stale emotions and expired events.

When we function from this mode of mind dominated by the "I-ego," we are out of sync with the integrity of the universal perspective and are working outside the realm of truth. We are then operating in a world of delusion founded on assumptions and projections of hopes that have no bearing whatsoever on our present reality. We could compare this abnormal situation to our computer screen saver. The idealized image with which we choose to decorate our monitor seems to have all the elements of reality, but it is not really connected anywhere "live." It is just a lifelike façade. Yet we are continually being fooled into believing it is real.

One of life's ironies is that the more time we spend becoming "educated," be it in a university or vocational school, the more we forget that we are all extraordinarily intelligent beings to begin with. The conditioning to which we have been, and continue to be, subjected by our social environment (including our parents, relatives, mentors, politicians, celebrities, and so forth) simply reinforces the myth that mental prowess is Nature's unique gift to its favored few. So we go through the motions of this lifetime totally oblivious to our innate brilliance and without confidence and trust in our natural abilities. It is not surprising, then, that we often feel so overwhelmed at the challenges we face, thinking that they are simply beyond the reach of our capabilities. If we are looking to improve our present circumstances, we need to keep in mind that as "part owners" of that infinite reservoir of wisdom-knowing we have the means to accomplish much more than we ever dreamed of. This connection to the divine realm is our birthright as human beings. Just pause and reflect on the profoundness of this thought for a moment.

Each one of us has as much access as anyone else does to the Mother-source, or what might aptly be called the "Universal Mind." Looking around us and seeing the disparity among people's predicaments may lead us to doubt this concept. We might ask ourselves how an unfortunate beggar living in a makeshift, cardboard tent in a back alley can be even remotely connected to you or to me, much less to someone like Bill Gates. But the saying that "we are all one" is not merely an esoteric aphorism. It is a simple fact by virtue of our common connection to the Universal Mind. Having access to the Universal Mind doesn't depend on anything we do. It is not as if the more material success we have gained, the bigger our share of that infinite power source will be. The divine connection I'm talking about is inherent in each of us, without exception, as soon as we assume humanity at birth.

Imagine our response if we were to receive the news that we had just inherited a considerable amount of money from a rich relative. I'm sure that this new state of financial freedom would give us confidence, ease of mind, and a more enthusiastic attitude toward life. Similarly, our connection to divine consciousness is like having an unlimited source of wealth in our bank account! As incredible as it may sound, we only need to access that wealth, at any time we choose, to improve our lives. How could the news be any better? We have to keep reminding ourselves of our tremendous legacy. We have infinite abundance simply waiting to be utilized. How to unlock the vault of this unimaginable wealth is what this book intends to show.

But first we need to understand our relationship with this Universal Mind. I would like to present some descriptive images and terminology to give you as close an idea as possible of the profound mind and its nature—what we might call the mind-behind-the-mind, the "other" mind, the source consciousness, or the Mother-mind.

However, at this point I must put in a caveat regarding the possibility of describing the mind and its contents. Here we encounter the problem of defining an indefinable idea. But for now, we have to resort to our limited human vocabulary, since conventional words are the only tools available to us. We therefore must take into careful account that words such as *corner*, *above*, or any other descriptive terms denoting physical dimensions are not intended to point to a physical reality. The mind is not of a physical nature.

Trying to describe the Universal Mind is similar to asking the eye to describe itself. There is an inherent difficulty because there is nothing behind this mind that could observe it from any distance. It is unobservable because it is the observer itself. It is simultaneously both everything and nothing. In the end, all we can say is that the profound Universal Mind is stateless, as it contains and incorporates all possible states. It is the fountainhead of life, the source of reality.

But even though we cannot accurately express in words the nature of this concept, we can do one better by *being* it. We can engage this state directly by overriding the mundane mind. We can access it by being present, right here, right now.

It is only in this expanded mentality that we can be fully in our lives and so be poised and capable of facing the enormous environmental challenges that stare us in the face. Already we see frightening and complex problems—the current wars, the economy, the state of health care, global warming—begging for creative and just solutions. Many more will come as the twenty-first century steams along. Our small, mundane mind is utterly inadequate and helpless in dealing with these challenges. For us to try to solve such immense problems from our own narrow perspective is similar to an ant trying to survey an elephant. The effort is an exercise in futility and will inevitably lead to frustration, confusion, chaos, and failure. Our confined, self-interested mind is overwhelmed by the scope of so many problems. It cannot see how the events in our lives are interrelated with the events in our world, and its instinctive reaction is to withdraw from issues that appear to be beyond our ability to resolve.

When we are able to access the Universal Mind, though, we enter a realm that vastly magnifies our active and accessible consciousness. It is only in this mode that we can have the unbiased perspective needed to deal with complex problems and challenges.

The Universal Mind is much more expansive than the ordinary mind, which is limited in forming ideas and making associations to the memory of personal experiences. This expansiveness is just one of the Universal Mind's many impressive qualities—qualities that manifest as they do because, here, we are at the source of our world, our life. When we open ourselves to the universal panorama of our higher level of consciousness, we are able to see that, while our ordinary mind is still occupied with the events of our everyday grind, at the same time we are out of and above it all.

In some enigmatic way, the Universal Mind encompasses the ordinary mind and is able to wrap around it as well. While these mind modes have always been linked together, the Universal Mind has remained largely undiscovered because of our distractions, preoccupations, and apathy. Our everyday world is fragmented and time bound, whereas the Universal Mind is free from the bondage of time, from self-consciousness, and from any specific location. More importantly, this dimension of the mind is free from fear. To live a life without fear is without a doubt an amazing achievement.

The exercises in this book of exploring the mind modes will greatly help us deepen our understanding of our human situation. Once we become familiar with the techniques for opening our mind beyond the ordinary and for expanding our awareness beyond the external world, we will develop the insight that defines the value of life. Only then will wisdom begin to unfold automatically. The more we cultivate wisdom, the smarter beings we will become.

Along with this development comes a noble and selfless spirit of compassion, a facet of wisdom manifesting. As this spirit enriches and nurtures our heart, we begin to live in a more loving and harmless manner, intuitively making the appropriate and humane choices vital to the survival of our ecosystem and the human race itself. This skillful use of our profound intelligence will allow us to enjoy and appreciate all that this life span offers us. If we take a few quiet moments to contemplate this thought, we will realize that in order to progress and prosper in peace, we must respond to the challenges of our times, not from a state of fear and anxiety, but from a state of circumspection—from a brightened mind.

The Universal Mind

Let us begin by acknowledging and examining human intelligence and recognizing what a truly awesome experience it is to be conscious and to possess intelligence. We have become so accustomed to the faculty of intelligence that we no longer see it for what it is, just as we have become accustomed to breathing and no longer appreciate that breath is life itself. We can count on it without any conscious effort to keep it going. Overfamiliarity with anything, regardless of its value, tends to diminish the focus of our attention on that subject, because we feel secure of its predictable presence in our life. This phenomenon causes us to overlook the remarkable assets we have as human beings. Let us try to understand this observation better.

Our mind has the genius to allocate many levels of priorities according to its own unique classification system within a field of infinite variables. It prioritizes subjects according to the degree of urgency they pose to our survival or security. It rearranges things into levels of acknowledgment so that the lowest priorities are set aside, relegated to the most remote sector of consciousness furthest from the present moment of awareness. The mind is always constantly prepared to respond to any crisis or emergency—it's always on the edge and ready for action, so to speak. If whatever it perceives does not fall into the top-priority category of "threat," the mind will automatically classify it under "future consideration," which in turn is further subdivided into several categories of priorities.

Using breath again as an example, when we catch a cold, our breathing becomes impaired, and air does not flow as easily as it normally does. This condition will instantly demand our attention. Within a split second, the mind will recognize the impairment as a potential threat to our survival and immediately reclassify breathing from a low to the top priority. It will then direct the rest of the human system to respond to the urgent task of unblocking the nasal passages so that life-giving oxygen can circulate more efficiently throughout the body. This process occurs continuously in our body at any given time throughout the course of our life.

Another amazing phenomenon is how our awareness can penetrate into our mind and perceive the marvelous, infinite variations that constitute it. When we go beyond ordinary consciousness, we can psychologically turn around and observe the state of that smaller mind. This is yet another unique attribute of the human consciousness—the ability to be reflective. It enables us to think and to experience mental, emotional, and physical experiences and, at the same time and from a higher level, to be aware that something is happening apart from this awareness. That is to say, we are cognizant of an overriding awareness that encompasses a smaller field of awareness. What's more, we are conscious of this consciousness.

This reflective attribute of the Universal Mind is unique to the human species. Its nature is to be that which stands apart, allowing it the perspective of being reflective. As the ultimate observer, it is detached and uninvolved in its subject of observation. It is this "stand-apart" quality or objectivity that distinguishes the supremacy of human intelligence over animals. Without this attribute we can only react in the most basic way, devoid of deep spiritual experiences. Imagine not being able to feel the expansive joy of generosity, compassion, wisdom, gratitude, and all other finer, subtler experiences. It is this reflective ability we tap into when faced with problems that are intrinsic to social interaction among fellow humans, at work, at school, or in the classroom of our life—challenges such as boredom, frustration, dullness, disappointment, laziness, and the tendency to make mistakes. All these can be investigated, processed, and resolved by the reflective mind. In fact, it is only in this way that we can grow and mature.

Every now and then we instinctively go beyond the everyday, mundane mind to retrieve information. This is what occurs each time some inexplicable insight or out-of-the-blue gut feeling arises. We call such insight *intuition*. The ordinary mind doesn't know where it comes from, because, whatever it is, it isn't constructed from material stored in our memory warehouse. And intuition is not rational, so it doesn't conform to human logic.

In fact, though, intuitive flashes come to us from the all-encompassing invisible energy field of the Universal Mind. These occurrences can give us an inkling of what we will encounter when we finally break through our ordinary way of thinking. A brightened mind is like being in a state of a sustained, intuitive flash.

In the practical context of day-to-day activities, the Universal Mind is the wellspring from which spontaneous recall arises. We've all experienced this connection with it at one time or another. It is familiar to us as that "ah-ha!" moment, when things we've been trying to sort out finally fall into perfect place with a satisfying click.

The Universal Mind is a veritable unending source of energy. It has the vitality to respond to life's issues however they unfold. It has the flexibility and virtue to recognize errors (that is, anything that violates universal laws) and to correct them. It has the fearless courage to turn things around—even upside down—in order to see things as they really are. The Universal Mind is accountable to no one and nothing but the highest truth.

Without a doubt, the link we have to this resource is our primary asset as human beings. Yet very few people truly appreciate the significance of this awesome, evolutionary legacy. Recognizing this gift is critical to our lives because, if we don't use all our intelligence in accordance with its natural design and purpose, life will be a constant, painful struggle. If we are not aware of possessing this great asset, we won't comprehend the means we have to help others. We will miss out on the joy of giving, and, instead, we will live with a sense of regret and guilt. More importantly, we will not be capable of right understanding, of seeing things as they really are, and of using this insight to alleviate our own suffering.

The Need
for Spiritual Education

The word *education* is derived from the Latin verb *educare*, meaning "to pull upward" or "to lead out." It has to do with pulling the mind out of the darkness of ignorance and into the light of knowing and understanding. Learning or "pulling ourselves upward" can be a lifelong and mind-expanding journey that can bring meaning to all we do. However, if all we are pursuing is academic or rote learning, we will end up shortchanging ourselves, for that mode of learning is empty of spirit. It does not teach us the values that will help us handle the daily challenges that we will all encounter in the course of our life.

It is for this reason that so many people are urging radical changes to the current educational system. Parents, sophisticated teachers, and the more evolved administrators are protesting the loss of a sense of sacredness in education. Here in Thailand, parents are eager for their sons to ordain as monks in their neighborhood *wat* (or "temple"), even if only for a few months. It is their hope that the time spent under the monks' guidance will provide a spiritual foundation in their children's lives and pave the way to a happy future for them. They are astute enough to recognize that spiritual values are essential in the development of their children into more refined, worthier human beings.

When education offers a balanced curriculum of academic and spiritual teaching, meaningful knowledge is conveyed. It is this aspect of education that gives meaning beyond material life and therefore bears the enduring legacy of what education is all about. This kind of learning pulls us upward beyond the simple acquisition of information to the development of wisdom.

Even centuries ago, our wise elders, particularly of the Eastern tradition, had long known of and practiced spiritually-based techniques to tap our intelligence reserves without cramming masses of information into our brains. If we would simply use these time-tested practices they have so generously passed on, we could save ourselves the fortune spent on researching so-called "smart genes" and the formula for reproducing intellectual genius.

But instead, our modern society insists on taking the scientific route with education. We are obsessed with the miniscule aspect of intelligence that can be measured in terms of IQ. Modern educational systems thus emphasize rational and linear intelligence involving logic. IQ tests indicate the speed, memory capacity, and mathematical abilities of our rational intellect. However, these tests do not weigh in the factors of emotional sensitivity, self-awareness in the present moment, and the subtle, intuitive capabilities of the Universal Mind. While modern education trains students to deal with mathematical equations and language construction, it does not begin to train the human mind to open beyond the severely limited and spiritually-confined boundaries of rationality.

Most Western-oriented schools all over the world teach children principles drawn from the beliefs and opinions of their school founders. These beliefs are then used as the premise for the school's educational curriculum. Right from the starting point, parameters in the educational system are established as the operational standard for future generations of students. The results of this well-intended but misguided structure are far reaching and profound and will affect the entire system throughout its existence. If the founding principles are based on ignorance or erroneous information, anything formulated around their premise will necessarily be a form of delusion. Regardless of the intention, such a system will miss the point of education altogether. It is this kind of teaching process—built solely on developing rote memory, personal beliefs, conjectures, and opinions—that produces what we could call a "diploma dummy." After years of accumulating information under this system, the only thing students have to show for it is a piece of parchment paper that is socially accepted as the validation of their efforts. In spite of this stamp of approval, these students still won't know much about themselves and therefore will never live up to their true potential. This is how our modern educational system produces future generations of weak-minded, politically oblivious, self-indulgent consumers.

Because the end result of an educational system that misdirects its students is inadequate, we can only expect more and more fat, drug dependent, unhappy people in the world. The inevitable outcome will be not only unfortunate but spiritually tragic. There will be fewer and fewer sensitive and clever people able to see beyond the parameters of the system. By the time students get their degrees, they will know just about everything there is to know about the Internet, the alcohol content of every brand of beer, the positive and negative factors of every smart phone, the telecast times for the most popular reality programs, and the air fares to Las Vegas and Disneyland. They will work and live for money in order to reach a physically secure retirement. Time will devour the opportunity life offers to look within, to search for the Truth. Without the inner exploration of the-way-things-are, life is destined to end in regret.

My intention in writing this book is to encourage you to expand your boundaries, so that such a story will not be yours. For one thing, you could enrich your life by reading the biographies of people like Mahatma Ghandi, Martin Luther King, Jr., the great spiritual lights of India, and, especially, the Buddha. More immediately, you can begin this expansion right now, in the present moment, using the conditions and situations of your own existence. Look within. Notice your emotions and mood changes.

For instance, notice that in the morning we usually feel rather dull and unambitious. In the afternoon, our mood is usually controlled by the power of wanting—wanting to go shopping, wanting to do something creative, wanting . . . something else. In the evening, we switch into a mode that searches for sensual pleasure: eating, going to a movie, watching TV, sending and receiving e-mails, and so on. Few people want to go to a movie at nine in the morning!

Learning to notice these overarching, mood-defining energies will help us become more aware of when we are happy, unhappy, confident, hesitant, worried, fearful, etc. We will become more conscious of feeling happy about meeting a friend, as opposed to feeling less than happy when meeting someone we don't like. Be honest with yourself. See things as they are, and your awareness will blossom.

Mind-Training Exercises

Let's explore the concept of the Universal Mind on a more practical level. Using the following meditation experiments, you will be able to see for yourself that the Universal Mind is always available to you. It is always ready to produce unlimited creativity and boundless innovative thinking, and always ready to bring a whole new dimension to your work or studies. Meditation, particularly the kind that is used in Buddhist practice, can produce an automatic upgrade in brain gigabytes that you never would have imagined was possible. At this point, take a few minutes to follow this technique in order to get a taste of the deep, abiding peace that you can access anytime, anywhere. It's yours for the asking.

Focus on Breathing

First, put your mind at ease. Turn off the rolling documentary of your past and future, at least for the duration of this experiment. Once you've done so, focus on a neutral object that will serve as your home base. This is the point to which you will return every time your mind gets lured into involvement with the past or the future. The most suitable neutral object used by most accomplished meditators is the breath, or the process of breathing—inhaling and exhaling. It is a simple and regularly occurring action of your body, so you don't need to go further than your nostrils to observe your chosen meditation object. Just keep your attention gently locked into the present moment, one breath at a time. Don't be tempted to gauge what happened two, three, four breaths ago or wonder if you can sustain your focus two breaths from now. That's not the present. Just stay with what is happening right in the moment. That's all.

If you want to be bolder with your foray into meditation, try holding one inhalation for as long as you can. Notice that during those seconds when nothing else is happening—when you are not even breathing—your mind is totally empty, devoid of any thought or any movement. Even in those few seconds, you immediately feel the presence of serenity and peace. It's as if you've parted the heavy drapes of your room to allow the sunshine to brighten it; the sun had been there all along, but you never noticed its presence until you chose to let it in. In this brightened room, which we can use as a metaphor for our mind, we are able to see objects more clearly. When the brightened mind is in a state of sustained stillness, it simply settles into a pure sense of knowing, a prelude to *vipassana*, or insight into the way things really are.

When you've come this far in the meditation experiment, you have disengaged yourself from the limitations of conventional time and have started operating in the boundless field of possibilities. You might even have surprised yourself to learn that you've sat in stillness for longer than you had expected. And for that much time, you've actually experienced a taste of true freedom. Thus, through concentration, you are able to free yourself from the body and the mundane, I-ego mind.

Preparing the Body and the Mind

The following instructions on how to make contact with the Universal Mind will enable you to use this higher level of consciousness to deal with your daily challenges and improve your learning ability.

First, prepare yourself to use your mind in a new way. Conduct this exercise while sitting comfortably. Allow your eyelids to close gently and begin to think "soft." That means relaxing the mind and smiling within. Let a smile lighten your face by simply relaxing your mouth and chin. Your lips will spread outward and form a smile. This won't happen by trying to *do* something; rather, it is a way of *undoing* and letting go into the smile. This smile brings us back to our natural innocence. This is our most natural look.

Then bring your attention to your body posture. You should lean slightly forward on your seat so as not to slump against a backrest.

As you become aware of your body, coaxing it to its natural state, you will become aware of your mind, for the body and the mind are intimately connected. You will feel yourself relaxing when you notice your breath lengthening and deepening. As you deepen your breath and allow it to return to its longer cycle, you will feel even more relaxed. Without forcing your breath to deepen, you will feel your chest expand further, and your lungs will take in more air.

As the chest expands, the rib cage opens and moves slightly upward; the movement of the floating ribs can be felt as well. The head, too, will tilt up a bit. If you are paying careful attention, you will feel your shoulders drop and the back muscles associated with your shoulders shift slightly. The body is coming back to a balanced state. This is a settling down into the natural alignment of the body that occurs when you are not feeling tense and anxious.

Let the face muscles and jaws relax a bit more. In fact, you can just allow gravity to relax the body from the top of the head all the way down to the soles of the feet. Take your time during this initial phase so that you can actually feel the tension and strain slip away. Experience the body and mind relaxing and softening as you go through the mind. Let your smile shine back into the mind. As we know, the mind can get too serious and can tighten up, just like the body does when it experiences stress. This smile is a biological signal; it stimulates softening "chemistry" that then reminds the body and mind to lighten up. It is important for us to turn our attention toward the body and thereby rejuvenate our awareness of it. We need to be with our body always if we want to be wholly present in our lives.

In time, as you gain more experience in training the body and mind to relax, you will go through this preparation stage rather easily. You will also continue to learn more and more about the inner feeling of what comes from tension and how to let go of it. Letting go is the most effective way to release both body and mind tension. When the body and mind are free of anxiety-related tension and stress, they can function in a smoother, more flexible and fluid manner. When the body has opened and extended back to its natural state, the mind will follow and respond accordingly.

In a moment, I will ask that you prepare the interior of your mind by breathing in the word *calm*. But first, let me explain what I mean by "breathing in" a word.

We breathe in a word by mentally inclining toward it with a silent whisper as we inhale. Consider that every word has power. Every word, even if we do not speak it but simply think of it, emits a vibration in our mind. When we mentally form the word *calm*, for instance, the vibration is such that the mind naturally inclines toward serenity. Soon the hard edge that is associated with thinking softens. A freeing sense of relaxation suffuses the mind, which deepens as we simply stay with the sensation that arises from the word *calm*.

This effect is cumulative. Every time we breathe in a word like *calm* or *tranquil*, the previous positive feelings we associate with that word reinforce our present action, with the result that inner light and a brightened mind are increasingly produced. Thus, the mind becomes progressively happier. And a mind that is happy is one that can easily concentrate.

Now, please begin to breathe in the word *calm*. As you are breathing, actually feel the effect that calmness has on the mind. Let a sense of calm saturate your being. Do this as best you can, breathing in *calm* without judging or doubting your ability to do so. Each of us is different and will experience this practice in our own way. But everyone who works with it will benefit from the results.

Next, breathe in the word *clear*, just as you did the word *calm*. Do this breathing exercise three times. Finally, breathe in the word *beyond* three times. Remember to keep smiling through this exercise. Loosen, open, and expand.

These instructions complete the preliminary exercises, which you can do wherever you happen to be.

Recent scientific experiments confirm that such active focus on a word is just as effective as actual physical movement for maintaining present-moment awareness. This awareness is essential for giving our practice true spiritual value, and, as we maintain it, we incline toward genuine meditation.

When you have been doing the relaxation exercises in earnest long enough to develop a modest amount of concentration on a meditational object, you are prepared to go on to the next step.

The Mind-Fitness Technique

Practicing the above breathing technique at home is all well and good, but you can gain additional experience by trying it in all kinds of situations. You can practice relaxation in this way even in a crowded room, or while sitting on a bus, or wherever you may be. I have many students who found they could use this technique to stay interested and alert, for instance, not only in a formal classroom setting but also in business meetings, or when waiting in a line, or when negotiating the terms of a rental contract.

When you follow this simple technique, over time your mind will begin to function more sharply and rapidly. You will be able to comprehend concepts and to grasp subtle aspects that you never noticed before. You will also find yourself being able to proceed with more confidence and enthusiasm. Let's see how it works:

First, plan to focus on a figure that you can follow for a period of time. Let's say, for example, that you are a student in a class. Begin by bringing all of your attention toward your instructor. Look at him from the moment he enters the room. Observe all his movements as carefully and closely as you can. Observe them so as to be able to write a precise report of his activities down to the smallest detail, as if you were doing a study on human behavior and this was the first instructor you had ever met. Your observation should be an applied one, which scans the whole space with a fascinated scrutiny that measures the present moment accurately and precisely.

When the instructor stands, note that activity. When he walks, note that as well. When he picks up the chalk, be aware of that. When he turns to the board to write something, be with those actions. As he writes on the board, observe how he forms each letter or each number. Take note of when he turns to look at you, when he puts the chalk down, where he puts it down. Notice his mouth moving and making sounds, his eyes scanning the class for clues that either he is being understood or that everyone is mostly shifting about in bewilderment. Patiently observe whatever is happening in the present moment.

Note each sequence of things as it occurs. When the instructor sits down, notice as he reaches for his chair how he moves and settles his body into the seat. Note everything, even the act of leaning back in the chair, gesturing with his hands, or calling on someone for an answer to a question. By focusing in this particular, concentrated manner, you are well aware of what the instructor is speaking about, and your mind is following his train of thought as he instructs the class. This astute listening comes about because your attention and the instructor's actions are so close together that they almost become one and the same.

In relaxing into this awareness, you are learning how to link the outside with the inner world. As this skill develops, you'll be surprised to discover that your awareness has gained a fluid, dynamic quality. This mode of natural-mindedness comes through as sensitive, sharp, and spontaneous. It is no longer rigidly fixed in the same, dull patterns to which we have become accustomed. Surprisingly, you are now more aware of what the instructor is saying than when you were just sitting passively in your chair with your mind adrift, feeling bored and waiting and hoping for the time to pass.

At all times, you should endeavor to sit in an alert posture, close to your writing surface, so that you can jot down whatever is necessary. When you write, bring the same precise attention to your own hand as it picks up the pen to form letters and words. Do not let your attention droop when you have to look away from the instructor. Then, when you have completed an entry, let your attention spring right back to your instructor. Let this attention be precise and formfitting, attached to the movements of the instructor, not lagging behind or floating adrift. In this way, you become present not only to what is around you (your body and your surroundings), but also to what is going on within you.

To maintain the momentum of focused attention, simply review at home what you have done in the world today. You will find that you will feel lighter and at ease with your day-to-day activities and learning experiences, eager to review the events of the day while they are still quite fresh and alive for you. When you come up against something you don't understand, make a note of it. Just that. Don't spend too much time worrying or thinking about it. Simply carry on reviewing and making notes to yourself to pursue what is not yet clear.

Because you have approached your study of a new skill methodically and as a kind of meditation (focusing your attention and being interested in the material, with the intention to increase your understanding), all the difficult aspects will eventually sort themselves out in the subconscious as you are doing other things. While you review your notes from working with your instructor, the things you already understood will have gone deeper, and the parts you have yet to understand will begin to unravel themselves in the back of your mind.

You could, of course, practice the same exercise with an employer, a coworker, or anyone else from whom you are trying to learn. Regardless, this is the way to keep the mind focused continuously on your task at hand. Even when you are relaxing and having fun with friends, this continuous attention will go on automatically just below the threshold of ordinary consciousness. The prime factor is our resolve to do well in everything we do. From that point on, the mind will gather focus and stability and launch itself into the process without conscious effort from you. Once good causes are established, good effects must follow.

Many learning experiences proceed something like this: At first, when presented with the unfamiliar, we may find ourselves mired in confusion. What is this all about? Where do I go from here? We then reflect on the dilemma in order to find something we can make sense of in it—or, at least, something vaguely familiar we can hold onto. Or perhaps we find something that our intuition tells us we are capable of thinking our way through. In any case, we shouldn't allow ourselves to be intimidated. We can learn anything by moving through the necessary steps, underpinning one level in order to progress to the next.

Actually, by reviewing the difficulties we've had in learning something new, we trigger the mechanism of memory that is lodged in the deeper levels of our consciousness. This layer of consciousness is the fountain of knowledge and wisdom I have described earlier as the Universal Mind. When we open up to it, our mind naturally becomes keener and brighter. Not only do we access our everyday knowledge, but we also provide the opportunity for creative insight of all sorts to come up into our mind and into our life.

That is all there is to this clever technique for mind fitness. You just need to observe keenly and continuously in this manner. Endeavor to maintain much of this alertness in all your day-to-day activities so that you have this technique close within and available to you. Then when you are in an actual situation that requires your full concentration, you will be prepared to gather your attention.

Endeavor to develop this technique through several weeks and months without looking for special results. These will come in their own good time. The most important and interesting special effect will be the recognition that you have entered the state of being in the moment. In abiding there, you will intuitively feel that this way of being is the most invigorating and satisfying mode of consciousness you have ever known.

When your mind has been developed this way, no matter what anyone asks you, you will be able to respond well immediately. Probably you will even discover that there will be many instances and situations when you will intuitively know what someone is about to ask even before he or she speaks. And your brightened mind, now linked with the Universal Mind, will open to the answer almost instantly as it flashes into your consciousness, even before the first words of the question are uttered.

Those of you who energetically and enthusiastically follow these instructions will soon find yourselves excelling in everything you do. From then on, you will be able to use this technique as a platform for broader, deeper exploration into your intuitive mind.

The simple exercise that you've just practiced will have given your mental and physical faculties a potent recharging. This is by far the most effective, proven way to develop a more dynamic, creative, and nimble mind that lives freshly in the moment. Just imagine the tremendous benefits if you were to practice this exercise regularly for an extended period of time. You would be continuously operating with the inexhaustible resources of the Universal Mind.

———

At this point, we now have an inkling of the magnificent piece of power equipment with which we were born—the mind. It is only natural that we would be interested in how it operates so that we can utilize its power for our benefit. In order to do so, we need to use the effective technique of training the mind with concentration. Concentration can enter only through silence and through the meditation techniques discussed earlier. External and internal stillness allows concentration to work its wonders of focusing our attention. In fact, this present-moment focus is the key to penetrating the understanding of anything and everything. Through concentration, the mind will harness itself and other diverging energies into one space once we direct it to our main objective. We can reach deeper realms than we could ever have fathomed with our ordinary thinking. We can then enter the domain of the Universal Mind.

In this state of deep concentration, the contents of the mind (objects, moods, thoughts, memories, feelings, etc.) take on a light and translucent quality, allowing us to investigate these elements without getting stuck in any of them. With this discerning detachment, we can see them for what they are: ever-changing energy patterns that don't belong to anyone and certainly are not ours to keep. In this brightened state, the mind can meet any situation with intelligent poise and composure.

We can develop this invaluable skill of present-moment awareness through regular practice, and, as we pay more attention to our mind, we will see that it holds a potential for seeing things we never imagined existed within ourselves.

Long-term success in life cannot be achieved simply by putting all our efforts into studying or working harder and longer so that we can earn a piece of paper certifying our accomplishments or an extra paycheck. It is sheer folly to depend on something or someone outside ourselves to validate our inner worth. Remember that everything of this world is subject to change. To rely on something that is fleeting is to put ourselves in the same predicament as a dog chasing its own tail.

What we can do is to know for ourselves and fully appreciate that we already possess a platinum field of inner intelligence into which we can link at any moment we choose. When we see deeply into the mind, we can experience the subtle and extraordinary perspective that the sages in every spiritual tradition have talked about. But to achieve this, we can rely only on our own power and no one else's. Once we are hooked into this expanded consciousness source, we might say that we are fully online.

Summary

With this new perspective and understanding of our connection with the Universal Mind, we can now utilize the information we have gained as we go about our daily lives. Whether we are in an office setting or a classroom or simply taking a walk down the street, we can implement this technology to make our minds far more efficient and productive. All we need to do is help ourselves to this profound field of consciousness that is freely available to every one of us without exception.

Let us summarize the extraordinary qualities of a brightened mind that is plugged into the power source, the Universal Mind:

- Expanded awareness: a dramatic upgrade of perspective from linear to multidimensional, which is somewhat like switching your vantage point from a peephole to a super-wide-screen panorama.

- Vibrant energy: a sustained dynamic power charge that generates fresh spontaneity and alertness of mind.

- Profound insight: the ability to evaluate situations with a depth of understanding born out of self-realization.

- Keener intelligence: the ability to respond to any life experience in an all-encompassing, holistic manner, and the ability to develop the life skills appropriate in a fully matured human being. This intelligence is a perfectly balanced energy emanating equally from the heart and the mind, imbued with wisdom and compassion.

- Cool imperturbability: the ability to be untouched by neurotic influences and emotions and to maintain an attitude of dynamic calmness.

- Flowing creativity: the ability to generate innovative, fresh ideas consistently from both new and old experiences as a result of an expanded awareness.

- Sharpened accuracy: the ability to reduce one's tendency to make mistakes, making it possible for goals to be carried out with quicker speed and with greater precision and efficacy.

- Enhanced sensitivity: the ability to communicate from the heart and make oneself understood without having to rely on ordinary vocabulary.

- Fearlessness: the ability to act with self-confident poise, knowing that it operates within the premise of truth unencumbered by doubts and mental constructs.

- Heightened attractiveness: the perceivable manifestation of all the above qualities in one individual that exudes a unique allure and irresistible charisma.

Now that you've been introduced to the real possibility of a brightened mind and shown the way to it, the final switching on of the power connection still lies in your hands. You now have the necessary information needed to accomplish this connection, but you must provide the interest, space, and time.

These are your options: you can spend your lifetime simply learning all the theories you want, or you can learn just the theories you need and spend the rest of your life putting them into action, living and enjoying them.

In pursuing an inner understanding of the Universal Mind, we learn more and more about what it means to be in this world as a human being. Our whole individual world actually arises out of our attitudes, moods, and the stuff that runs through our heads. If we can come to understand how these inner factors relate to the outer world of experience, we can then come to understand how to live in a much wiser and more compassionate manner. Herein lies the key to a successful and happy life.

The Ultimate Goal

Needless to say, there is a lot to learn in this life. And whatever we can learn can only happen in a tiny time frame, just the time when there is still breath in our body. There is enough time, and yet we need to hustle, because we never know when our time will run out. If you just implement what you have been reading in this book, you will have an excellent tool for learning life's most important lessons while you have the opportunity to do so. And you will be in a position to develop the more highly regarded human qualities that are admired universally. From an

Eastern spiritual perspective, this development is what we enter into life to attain.

While the emphasis here has been on developing a quiet mind (*samadhi*) in order to relax and to make the mind sharp and vigilant, there is an even bigger goal. That bigger objective is the development of the special qualities that transform us into sensitive, intelligent, and compassionate human beings and lead us toward enlightenment. When we mature in this way, we become less and less selfish and more and more energetic. We find that we are surrounded and encouraged by good, trustworthy, and helpful people (quality friends). Our life generates the boon that is the fuel for sharpening our inherent wisdom (quality mind). Discrimination and compassion are the essential qualities that beautify our life and make our life harmonious. With them we are able to sharpen our life skills, broaden our horizons, and interact with others in a more refined way. The qualities of discrimination, intelligence, and circumspect awareness—

really, good common sense—bring competence and enthusiasm into our life and help us select true friends. True friends respect us, look after us, and wish us well. "Good-time" friends just hang around looking for opportunities to exploit our relationship. *Good* friends, on the other hand, guide and support our highest potential because they love us and wish us the best, whereas self-seeking and foolish friends lead us into trouble. Without wisdom we can easily blunder into unhealthy associations. Look around and you will quickly verify this truth. Wisdom is the energy we can trust to guide our life toward our highest potential. It is the energy that strengthens vigilance. And vigilance protects us from sorrow.

My ultimate intention in writing this book has been to awaken your mind toward silent introspection: meditation—for meditation practice is the technique that generates a peaceful, transcendent mental environment. When the mind is inclined toward the peaceful, the ethical, and the beautiful (even in a world as dangerous and as selfish as this one), it will protect us, strengthen our weak points, and empower us. Meditation keeps us alert to the fact that, without awareness, we become victims of a restless mind, of overpowering emotions, and of our karmic propensities. It supports clear, intelligent thinking so that we find we are able to lift up our life rather than be drawn into the sort of heedless activities that are actually dark karmic forces with the ability to drag us down. These energies know just exactly how to exploit our weaknesses.

Wisdom is the superpower. It sees to it that we are not seduced into stupid activities. It provides us with an outlook from which to observe compulsive thoughts rather than be drawn into them. It protects us from selfish desires to exploit others or to escape from our responsibilities. This meditative mind maintains a vision for the future—a vision that can actualize our life energy into becoming everything we can be.

The good life (a spiritual life) arises along a path that can be cultivated. It is a path that calls us to be careful, disciplined, and aware. It involves the development of mindfulness in the present moment. This energy looks after us in every aspect of our daily life. It challenges our poor habits. For example, it is the supreme remedy for countering laziness and robotic activity. Meditation practices that concentrate the mind and bring focus to our world also prompt us to set up moderate discipline in our life. They help us recognize that we need this kind of boundary around our life in order to protect us from doing things we would regret. That boundary protects us from doubt and worry. It stays above the emotions, the negative thoughts, and the foolish ideas.

This inner development naturally leads us to find an occupation—a livelihood from which we earn money skillfully and appropriately—and teaches us how to use money so that it doesn't cause a problem for ourselves or for others. Our life becomes a living role model. The in-the-moment attentiveness of our life awakens others to live their lives more consciously. We act and live in a way that is of benefit to us as well as to others. The knowledge that we acquire in school and in books, along with our meditation practice, is used to develop our character, to mold us into loving, intelligent, truly human beings. We won't have wasted our opportunity to wake up and live the whole of our life.

In the end, being attentive and maintaining awareness, both in the external environment as well as in our interior mental environment, is the same intelligent attitude we need wherever we are. When we learn how to be fully present in our daily activities, we will know how to be present everywhere life takes us. Indeed, there is a lot at stake here.

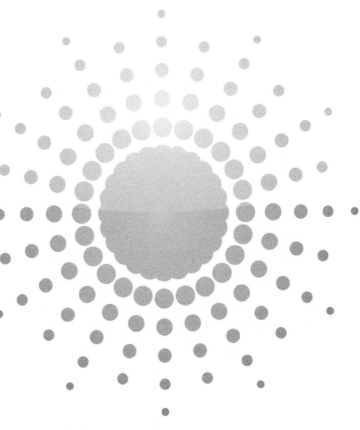

Contemplations
for the Reader

A Meditation on Loving-Kindness

These are the characteristics of those who are skilled in goodness and know the path of peace:

Let them be able and upright, straightforward and gentle in speech, humble and not conceited, contented and easily satisfied.

Let them be unburdened with duties and frugal in their ways; peaceful and calm; and wise and skillful, not proud and demanding in nature.

Let them not do the slightest thing that the wise would later reprove.

Let them wish in gladness and in safety, *may all beings be at ease!* Whatever living beings there may be—omitting none, whether they be weak or strong; the great or the mighty, the medium, the short, or the small; both the seen and the unseen, strangers and those known to us, those living near and far away, those born and to be born—*may all beings be at ease!*

Let them not deceive another or despise any being in any state.

Let them not through ill will or anger wish harm upon another.

Even as a mother protects with her life her child, her only child, so with a boundless heart let them cherish *all* living beings.

Let them radiate kindness over the entire world—spreading upward to the skies and downward to the depths, outward and unbounded, freed from hatred and malice.

Whether standing or walking, seated or lying down, let them sustain tranquility of mind, free from drowsiness.

Let all who aspire to loving-kindness remember: All actions are led by our own mind. Mind is the master. Act or speak with loving-kindness, and happiness will surely follow.

Reflections on Being

What am I becoming? Where am I heading? Do I see that the days and nights are flying quickly?

May I ever aspire toward goodness. May my life incline toward harmlessness.

May I be free of ill will. May I abandon foolish speech. May I sustain my life in a good and honest manner. May I use my time well.

What is past has been left behind. What is in the future has not yet arrived. Today I am alive. Tomorrow—who knows? Death may come, for death is certain while life is precarious. Today is all there is. There is only now.

All living beings strive to be free from all manner of suffering. All living beings are searching for security and happiness. I, too, seek to be free from suffering.

May all who are dear and have been kind to me, living or no longer living, be free from suffering. May they be happy and safe from harm. May all other beings—infinite, visible, and invisible—be free from all suffering and harm.

May I live in harmony and with ease. May I look after myself appropriately. May I not lose the goodness I have attained.

May all beings live in harmony and with ease. May all beings look after themselves appropriately. May all beings not lose the goodness they have attained.

May we all recognize that we are the owners of our actions, the heirs to our actions, and related to and dependent upon our actions. Whatever we do, be it good or harmful, its consequences will be ours.

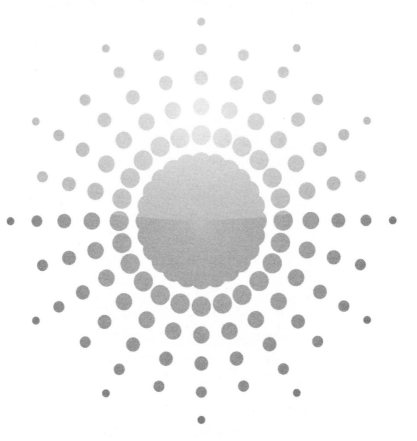

Affirmation of Spiritual Friendship

A spiritually sensitive person cultivates spiritual friendships.

A true spiritual friend always looks after my well-being, sharing in my sorrows and joys. She or he is sincere and empathetic. He or she points me toward that which is beneficial. She cautions me to avoid useless and hurtful conduct, the same old habitual mistakes, and variations of self-destructive behavior.

Spiritual friendship is a blessing in one's life.

That being so, I will enlighten my life. I will make my life a blessing to others.

I will be a spiritual friend.

About the Author

Ajahn Sumano Bhikkhu was born in Chicago, Illinois. He learned the essential truths concerning our mind . . . the hard way. All of his insight was absorbed and integrated through sitting at the feet of the great meditation masters of the twentieth century and by engaging in intense, passionate meditation for twelve years in a cave in northeastern Thailand.

Before ordaining twenty-five years ago, Sumano traveled and lived in various yoga, meditation, and Sufi communities. Before that, he lived the life of his American culture as a university, military, and government administrator; a conglomerate entrepreneur; a businessman; a Stanford researcher; and a world traveler.

At the age of twenty-nine, he retired and turned away from the distractions of the material world. He began a fitness regime, stopped smoking and drinking, and studied yoga, martial arts, and massage therapy. He spent several years devouring books in the libraries at Stanford University, trying to satiate his hunger to understand the nature of the human predicament: Why are we here? Why do we suffer? Is karma real? What really belongs to us? After thousands of hours pursuing the ideas of the outstanding intellects in the spheres of philosophy, psychology, comparative religion, and linguistics, he discarded that path, seeing that all of it led only to concepts, hypotheses, and beliefs.

Packing his backpack, Sumano set out on an eighteen-month trip around the world, where he experienced his first taste of the Orient and Buddhism. Returning to the United States, he tidied up unfinished business, said good-bye to friends and family, and headed back to India. Curiously, on a stopover in London, he met several disciples of the famous Buddhist meditation master in the Thai Forest Tradition, Phra Ajahn Chah Supatto, who had just arrived to establish a branch monastery in England. That stopover lasted seven years. Having become a forest monk himself, Sumano later journeyed to the northeast of Thailand, volunteering to serve as a caregiver to Phra Ajahn Chah, who had suffered a disabling stroke.

Sumano has lived at his cave sanctuary in Nakhon Ratchasima Province for fifteen years. He no longer leads retreats or receives guests but can be contacted through e-mail at monksumano@yahoo.com or www.next-life.com.

Quest Books

encourages open-minded inquiry into
world religions, philosophy, science, and the arts
in order to understand the wisdom of the ages,
respect the unity of all life, and help people explore
individual spiritual self-transformation.

Its publications are generously supported by
The Kern Foundation,
a trust committed to Theosophical education.

Quest Books is the imprint of
the Theosophical Publishing House,
a division of the Theosophical Society in America.
For information about programs, literature,
on-line study, membership benefits, and international centers,
see www.theosophical.org
or call 800-669-1571 or (outside the U.S.) 630-668-1571.

To order books or a complete Quest catalog,
call 800-669-9425 or (outside the U.S.) 630-665-0130.

Related Quest Titles

*Everyday Dharma: Eight Weeks to Finding the
Buddha in You*, by Lama Willa Miller

Finding the Quiet Mind, by Robert Ellwood

The Illustrated Encyclopedia of Buddhist Wisdom,
by Gill Farrer-Halls

The Meditative Path, by John Cianciosi

*Questions from the City, Answers from
the Forest*, by Ajahn Sumano Bhikkhu

A Still Forest Pool, by Jack Kornfield, with Paul Breiter